ANXIOUS ATTACHMENT RECOVERY - YOUR 90-DAY PATH FROM CLINGING TO CONFIDENCE

STOP OVERTHINKING EVERY TEXT, HEAL YOUR FEAR OF ABANDONMENT, AND CREATE LASTING INTIMACY WITHOUT PLAYING IT COOL

ELLIOT CHASE

CONTENTS

INTRODUCTION

You stare at your phone screen, the timestamp showing 11:47 AM. Your partner read your "Good morning!" text at 7:23 AM—four hours and twenty-four minutes ago. You know the exact time because you've checked forty-seven times in the past hour.

Each glance at your phone sends a fresh wave of anxiety through your chest. Maybe they're losing interest. Maybe you're too much. Maybe they met someone else. Your mind spirals through every possible catastrophe, each scenario more devastating than the last. You craft and delete seventeen different follow-up messages, oscillating between casual and desperate.

Sound familiar?

This exhausting cycle isn't a character flaw or emotional weakness. It's anxious attachment—a learned pattern that developed to help you survive, but now sabotages the very connections you crave most. The good news? It can be unlearned.

YOUR 90-DAY JOURNEY TO SECURE LOVE

This book exists for one powerful purpose: to guide you through a comprehensive 90-day transformation from anxious attachment to secure, confident love.

Too many people believe anxious attachment is a life sentence. That if you're "naturally" clingy, jealous, or overthinking, you're doomed to exhaust yourself and your partners with emotional turbulence. This book shatters that myth with scientific precision and compassionate guidance.

Your anxious attachment patterns didn't develop overnight, and they won't disappear with surface-level tips. Real transformation requires:

- Understanding the deep roots of your attachment system
- Challenging unconscious beliefs driving your behavior
- Systematically rewiring your nervous system's responses to love

This isn't about suppressing emotions or "playing it cool" to manipulate attraction. It's about achieving genuine emotional peace. Imagine going to sleep without replaying every interaction, looking for hidden signs of rejection. Picture yourself fully present in conversations instead of anxiously monitoring your partner's mood for threats.

WHO THIS BOOK IS FOR

This book is specifically designed for individuals who recognize themselves in anxious attachment patterns and are ready for deep transformation.

You might be the person who:

- Checks your phone obsessively after sending texts, analyzing response times for hidden meanings
- Feels physically ill when your partner seems distant, even for normal reasons like work stress
- People-pleases to avoid conflict, then resents losing your authentic self
- Experiences intense fear when relationships hit normal rough patches
- Oscillates between clingy desperation and angry withdrawal
- Knows intellectually your reactions are "too much" but feels powerless to change them

You're ready for this journey if you:

- Want to transform from reactive to responsive in your closest connections
- Can commit to 90 days of consistent daily practices
- Desire genuine intimacy built on security rather than desperate clinging born from fear
- Are willing to examine painful experiences that shaped your attachment style

This book will work whether you're single or partnered. These patterns appear in all relationships—romantic, friendship, family, and professional.

WHY THIS BOOK IS DIFFERENT

The relationship advice landscape overflows with surface-level tips and one-size-fits-all solutions. This book takes a fundamentally different approach.

Attachment Science Meets Practical Application

Every strategy is grounded in attachment research while providing concrete daily practices designed specifically for anxious attachment healing. You'll understand not just what to do, but why it works and how it rewires your nervous system.

Challenging the "Play It Cool" Myth

This book directly challenges the toxic cultural message that you must suppress your emotional nature to be attractive. Your capacity for deep feeling is a strength, not a weakness.

The goal isn't becoming emotionally distant, but emotionally regulated.

Integration of Multiple Healing Modalities

This comprehensive approach draws from attachment theory, neuroscience, somatic practices, cognitive behavioral techniques, and mindfulness traditions. You'll have a complete toolkit addressing mental, emotional, physical, and spiritual dimensions of attachment healing.

YOUR ROADMAP TO SECURE ATTACHMENT

This book guides you through three distinct phases, each building on the previous foundation.

Phase One: Understanding Your Origins (Days 1-30)

You'll compassionately explore how your attachment patterns formed through childhood experiences and family dynamics. This develops profound self-compassion by understanding why you developed these patterns initially. You'll identify specific triggers, map nervous system responses, and begin practicing basic emotional regulation.

Phase Two: Interrupting Current Patterns (Days 31-60)

With self-understanding as your foundation, you'll learn to catch anxious patterns in real-time and interrupt them with skillful responses. You'll practice present-moment awareness, nervous system regulation, and develop secure communication skills while experimenting with new responses in actual relationships.

Phase Three: Building Secure Patterns (Days 61-90)

The final phase focuses on consistently choosing secure responses until they become your new default. You'll deepen your capacity for authentic intimacy, maintain your sense of self within relationships, and develop skills for navigating conflict from secure foundations.

Throughout Your Journey, You'll Encounter:

- Daily practices designed to rewire your nervous system
- Detailed case studies showing different paths to transformation
- Multiple perspectives on major attachment healing topics
- Clear progress markers to recognize your growth

By the end of 90 days, you won't be a different person—you'll be the most authentic version of yourself, freed from exhausting anxious patterns. You'll maintain your capacity for deep love while gaining inner security that makes relationships sustainable and nourishing.

COMMIT TO YOUR TRANSFORMATION

Reading about attachment healing isn't the same as healing your patterns. These insights will only transform your life if you commit to implementing them consistently over the next 90 days.

Real change happens between knowing and doing.

The 90-day framework isn't arbitrary. Neuroscience research shows it takes approximately this long to form new neural pathways strong enough to compete with established patterns. Some days will feel like breakthroughs. Others will feel like moving backward.

Both are normal.

This journey will ask you to question beliefs about relationships you've held since childhood. You might discover that what you thought was love was actually fear, that what you believed was caring was actually controlling. This can feel destabilizing, but it's necessary for growth.

As you become more secure, your relationships will shift. Some will deepen as you bring more authenticity and less reactivity. Others might struggle as you stop playing familiar roles or tolerating unhealthy dynamics.

This isn't failure—it's alignment.

Your anxious attachment patterns have already cost you enough in emotional energy, relationship satisfaction, and peace of mind. Every day you delay this work is another day of exhausting overthinking, another day of relationship anxiety.

The time is now.

Before turning to Chapter 1, make this commitment real. Write down today's date and these words: "I commit to 90 days of consistent practice to transform my attachment patterns from anxious to secure."

Sign it.

Your secure, peaceful, authentic future self is waiting.

Let's begin.

1

THE ARCHAEOLOGY OF YOUR HEART - WHY YOUR PAST HOLDS TOMORROW'S KEYS

WHERE HEALING BEGINS

When Mary first walked into my office, she clutched her phone like a lifeline, checking it every few minutes for messages from her boyfriend. "I know I'm being crazy," she whispered, "but I can't stop myself from needing to know where he is every second." What Mary didn't realize was that her hypervigilance wasn't random—it was a perfectly logical response to a childhood where love came with conditions and disappeared without warning.

Understanding your attachment origins isn't about dwelling in the past or assigning blame; it's about recognizing the adaptive strategies your young mind created to survive emotional uncertainty. These patterns, formed in your earliest relationships, become the blueprint for how you navigate intimacy as an adult. The debate between addressing root causes versus present symptoms misses a crucial point: you can't fully transform what you don't understand.

The archaeological approach to healing reveals three key insights:

- Early patterns create neural pathways: Your brain literally wired itself around your first experiences of safety and connection, making certain responses feel automatic and unavoidable
- Present-focused approaches often provide temporary relief: While mindfulness and current-moment interventions help manage symptoms, they rarely address the underlying architecture of insecurity
- Integration offers the most sustainable healing: Combining historical understanding with present-moment awareness creates lasting transformation rather than surface-level coping

Benjamin spent years in therapy learning breathing techniques and cognitive restructuring to manage his relationship anxiety. While these tools helped him function better day-to-day, his core terror of abandonment remained untouched. It wasn't until he connected his fear of his partner leaving to watching his father walk out when he was seven that he could finally address the root of his desperate clinging.

Understanding his origin story didn't excuse his behavior. But it gave him clarity.

The excavation process requires patience and self-compassion. Your attachment system developed over years of repeated interactions, and healing happens in layers rather than sudden breakthroughs. As we move into exploring the neuroscience behind these patterns, remember that your brain's wiring isn't your destiny—it's simply your starting point for conscious transformation.

BORN THIS WAY OR MADE THAT WAY

Patricia often wondered if she was "born this way"—destined to be the anxious one in every relationship. Her mother had been clingy and possessive, her grandmother notorious for dramatic emotional outbursts when family members didn't call often enough. "Maybe it's just in my DNA," she'd say with resignation, as if her attachment style was an unchangeable sentence written in her genes.

The nature versus nurture debate in attachment theory has created unnecessary polarization between those who believe we're genetically predetermined and those who focus solely on environmental factors. The truth is far more nuanced and, ultimately, more hopeful. While we may inherit certain temperamental tendencies—like sensitivity to rejection or intensity of emotional response—our attachment patterns are primarily learned adaptations to our early caregiving environment.

The interplay between biology and experience reveals three crucial insights:

- Temperament provides the raw material: Some people are naturally more sensitive or emotionally reactive, creating a foundation that can develop into anxious attachment under certain conditions
- Environment shapes expression: Even highly sensitive children can develop secure attachment when their caregivers are consistently responsive and attuned to their needs
- Neuroplasticity means change is possible: Regardless of genetic predisposition or early conditioning, your brain remains capable of forming new neural pathways throughout your lifetime

William discovered this firsthand when he traced his family's attachment patterns across three generations. His grandfather had been emotionally distant after returning from war, his father had learned to equate love with achievement, and he had inherited a legacy of conditional affection. But recognizing these patterns as learned rather than inevitable gave him the power to break the cycle.

This revelation changed everything for him.

Through understanding his environmental conditioning, he could finally stop the exhausting cycle of overthinking every interaction with his partner and begin building the secure relationship he'd always craved. The archaeological dig through his family history revealed that his anxious attachment wasn't a genetic curse but a learned survival strategy that had outlived its usefulness.

As we prepare to examine the neurobiological evidence in our next chapter, remember this: your brain's current wiring reflects your past experiences, not your future possibilities. Understanding the courtroom where your neural networks make split-second decisions about love and safety will illuminate exactly how transformation becomes possible.

WHEN PAIN BECOMES PROTECTION

At age five, Sarah learned that when her mother got that distant look in her eyes, it meant she was about to disappear—sometimes for hours, sometimes for days. So Sarah became a master of reading micro-expressions, monitoring moods, and doing whatever it took to keep her mother engaged and present. What looked like a "difficult" or "needy" child was actually a brilliant survival strategist.

The traditional view of childhood wounds often pathologizes the very adaptations that helped us survive. But what if your anxious attachment patterns weren't evidence of damage, but proof of your remarkable ability to adapt and survive? This reframe doesn't minimize the pain of early experiences, but it honors the intelligence and resilience that got you through them. Your hypervigilance, your people-pleasing, your fear of abandonment—these weren't character flaws, they were sophisticated survival mechanisms.

Understanding your adaptive strategies reveals their original purpose:

- Hypervigilance as early warning system: Your ability to read subtle changes in others' moods and behavior developed as a way to predict and prevent emotional abandonment
- People-pleasing as connection insurance: Becoming indispensable to others felt like the safest way to ensure they wouldn't leave, even if it meant losing yourself in the process
- Emotional intensity as communication strategy: Big feelings got attention when subtle cues were ignored, teaching you that drama was sometimes the only path to connection

Marcus had always been ashamed of his "neediness" in relationships, constantly seeking reassurance and becoming clingy when his partner seemed distant. But when he reframed this pattern as an adaptation to having emotionally unavailable parents, everything shifted. His vigilance around his partner's moods wasn't pathological—it was the same skill that had helped him navigate his unpredictable childhood home.

This reframe changed his entire approach to healing.

Rather than trying to eliminate his sensitivity, Marcus learned to channel it more consciously and effectively. He transformed from clingy and desperate to confidently secure, not by suppressing his attachment needs, but by understanding their origins and finding healthier ways to meet them.

As we move into examining the neurobiological courtroom where these patterns operate, remember that your brain's protective mechanisms were designed to keep you safe. Understanding how these neural networks function will show you exactly how to redirect their power toward creating the secure relationships you've always desired.

YOUR HYPERVIGILANCE IS ACTUALLY WISDOM

Rachel could detect a shift in her partner's mood from across the room. She noticed when his texts became slightly shorter, when his goodnight kisses lasted half a second less, when his laugh didn't quite reach his eyes. Friends called her "paranoid," therapists labeled her "hypervigilant," but what if this exquisite sensitivity was actually a form of emotional intelligence that had been misunderstood and misdirected?

The pathology model of anxious attachment treats hypervigilance as a disorder to be eliminated rather than a skill to be refined. But people with anxious attachment often possess remarkable abilities: they're highly attuned to others' emotional states, deeply empathetic, and capable of incredible loyalty and devotion. The problem isn't the sensitivity itself—it's how we've learned to use it and what we do with the information it provides.

Your heightened sensitivity contains hidden gifts:

- Emotional radar as relationship asset: Your ability to sense subtle changes in relationship dynamics can be incredibly valuable when channeled toward understanding rather than catastrophizing
- Empathy as superpower: Your deep capacity to feel what others feel makes you an exceptional friend, partner, and supporter when you're not drowning in your own anxiety
- Intensity as passion: The same emotional intensity that creates relationship drama can fuel incredible creativity, deep connections, and meaningful experiences when properly directed

Thomas learned to see his relationship anxiety not as a weakness to overcome, but as misdirected intelligence to be refined. Instead of using his emotional sensitivity to scan for signs of rejection, he began using it to build genuine intimacy. He learned to trust his perceptions while questioning his interpretations, to feel his feelings without being controlled by them.

This shift changed everything for him.

He discovered how to use his natural attunement to create deeper connection rather than desperate clinging. His hypervigilance became a tool for understanding his partner's needs instead of a source of constant worry about abandonment.

Your past isn't a prison—it's an archaeological site rich with information about how you learned to love and be loved. The nature versus nurture debate becomes irrelevant when you realize that regardless of your starting point, your brain's neuroplasticity means secure attachment is always possible. Your anxious patterns aren't evidence of brokenness but proof of your remarkable ability to adapt and survive.

As we move into the neuroscience courtroom, you'll discover exactly how your brain processes attachment information and why understanding these mechanisms is crucial for lasting transformation.

2

THE NEUROSCIENCE COURTROOM - YOUR BRAIN ON ANXIOUS ATTACHMENT

WHEN YOUR BRAIN TAKES THE WHEEL

Your amygdala doesn't care about your relationship goals—it only cares about survival. When anxious attachment patterns activate, this almond-shaped structure in your brain sounds alarm bells that can override your rational mind within milliseconds. The question becomes: are you a victim of your brain's ancient wiring, or can you learn to pause and choose your response?

From Chapter 1, we explored how your childhood experiences carved neural pathways that still influence your reactions today. Now we need to understand the actual mechanics of what happens inside your skull when those old wounds get triggered. Your brain operates like a courthouse where different systems compete for control.

The Neural Players in Your Attachment Drama:

- The amygdala: Your brain's smoke detector, scanning for relationship threats 24/7

- The prefrontal cortex: Your brain's CEO, capable of logical thinking and emotional regulation
- The hippocampus: Your memory bank, which can get hijacked during emotional floods
- The vagus nerve: Your internal communication highway between brain and body

The problem with anxious attachment is that your amygdala has been trained to see danger everywhere. When your partner doesn't text back immediately, your smoke detector screams "ABANDONMENT!" before your CEO brain can assess the situation rationally.

The 90-Second Rule

Neurobiologist Jill Bolte Taylor discovered that the chemical rush of emotions floods your system for exactly 90 seconds. After that, you're choosing to stay in the emotional loop.

This changes everything.

Prefrontal Cortex Override

Your brain's CEO can learn to recognize amygdala activation and engage the pause button, but only with consistent practice and awareness. The key is developing what psychologists call your "window of tolerance"—your capacity to stay present during emotional activation without flipping into fight-or-flight or freeze responses.

Isabella used to check her boyfriend's phone whenever anxiety spiked, convinced she'd find evidence of betrayal. She'd describe feeling "possessed" during these moments—her hands moving before her mind could intervene. Through mindfulness training, she learned to recognize the physical sensations that preceded her amygdala hijacks: tight chest, racing heart, tunnel vision.

Now when these signals arise, she practices the 90-second rule, breathing deeply and reminding herself: "This feeling will pass. I can choose my response."

Her relationship transformed when she stopped letting her amygdala make decisions for her heart. In Chapter 3, we'll examine how this neural drama plays out in your digital communications.

REWIRING LOVE AGAINST YOUR DNA

The great debate rages in neuroscience circles: are we prisoners of our early attachment experiences, or can we literally rewire our brains for secure connection? The answer lies somewhere between destiny and possibility, with neuroplasticity research showing that our brains remain remarkably changeable throughout our lives—but change requires specific conditions and sustained effort.

Remember those childhood patterns we excavated in Chapter 1? Your brain carved deep neural highways based on those early relationship experiences. But here's the revolutionary news: those highways aren't permanent superhighways. They're more like dirt roads that can be rerouted with enough traffic on new paths.

The Science of Neural Rewiring:

- Critical periods vs. sensitive periods: While early childhood creates deep neural pathways for attachment, these patterns remain modifiable throughout life, especially during times of significant emotional experiences
- Repetition and emotional salience: New neural pathways strengthen through consistent practice combined with emotionally meaningful experiences—you can't think your way into new attachment patterns
- The 10,000-hour myth: Attachment rewiring doesn't require a decade of therapy, but it does need consistent,

intentional practice over months and years to create lasting change

Your amygdala from our courthouse discussion earlier doesn't want to give up its hypervigilant job. It's been protecting you for years, scanning for abandonment threats with the dedication of an overworked security guard. Teaching it to relax requires patience and proof that safety is possible.

The Earned Security Revolution

Psychologists discovered something remarkable: adults can develop "earned secure attachment" regardless of their childhood experiences. This happens through corrective emotional experiences—relationships that provide consistent safety, attunement, and emotional regulation.

Joseph grew up with a mother who alternated between smothering attention and cold withdrawal. At thirty-five, he found himself recreating this pattern—desperately seeking reassurance from partners, then pushing them away when they got too close. His therapist introduced him to the concept of earned secure attachment, explaining how his brain could literally grow new neural pathways through corrective emotional experiences.

Through a combination of therapy, mindfulness practice, and consciously choosing relationships with securely attached partners, Joseph began noticing changes within six months. His brain scans after two years showed increased activity in areas associated with emotional regulation and decreased reactivity in his amygdala.

The neural courthouse we explored earlier can learn new rules. In Chapter 3, we'll examine how these brain changes play out in your digital communications.

DRAMA ADDICTION VS REAL LOVE

Your brain's reward system doesn't distinguish between healthy excitement and toxic drama—both trigger dopamine release that can become addictive. For those with anxious attachment, the intermittent reinforcement of push-pull relationships creates a neurochemical cocktail that feels like love but functions more like a slot machine, keeping you hooked on uncertainty rather than nourished by consistency.

This connects directly to those childhood patterns we uncovered in Chapter 1. If your early caregivers were unpredictable—sometimes loving, sometimes distant—your developing brain learned to chase the high of earning affection rather than expect the steady warmth of unconditional love.

Your neural courthouse from Chapter 2 gets hijacked by this drama addiction. The amygdala loves intensity because it feels important and alert. The prefrontal cortex knows better, but dopamine is a powerful drug that overrides rational thinking.

The Neuroscience of Drama Addiction:

- Intermittent reinforcement schedules: Unpredictable rewards like occasional affection from an avoidant partner create stronger addiction patterns than consistent positive reinforcement
- Dopamine vs. oxytocin pathways: Drama activates dopamine (wanting/craving), while secure attachment builds oxytocin (bonding/contentment)—learning to distinguish between excitement and genuine connection
- Tolerance and withdrawal: Like any addiction, relationship drama requires increasing intensity to achieve the same high, while stable relationships may initially feel "boring" as your brain adjusts to healthier reward patterns

The Slot Machine Effect

Think about it: slot machines don't pay out consistently. They hook players with unpredictable rewards that trigger massive dopamine surges. Your anxious attachment patterns work the same way. That partner who texts you sweet messages one day and goes silent the next? Pure intermittent reinforcement.

Diana realized she was addicted to relationship chaos when she found herself sabotaging a perfectly healthy relationship because it felt "too easy." She'd create arguments just to experience the rush of making up, or flirt with other men to trigger her boyfriend's jealousy and subsequent attention. Her therapist helped her understand that her brain had learned to associate love with intensity and uncertainty.

She had to consciously retrain her reward system to appreciate the subtle pleasures of secure attachment: morning coffee conversations, predictable goodnight texts, and the quiet contentment of being truly known. The transition felt like "emotional detox"—boring at first, then deeply nourishing as her oxytocin pathways strengthened.

In Chapter 3, we'll explore how this drama addiction plays out specifically in your digital communications.

REWRITING MEMORIES TO HEAL TRAUMA

Every time you recall a memory, your brain briefly returns it to a malleable state where it can be updated with new information. This process, called memory reconsolidation, offers a powerful pathway for healing attachment wounds—but it requires more than just talking about the past. True healing happens when old memories are activated in the presence of new, corrective emotional experiences.

Think back to those childhood patterns we excavated in Chapter 1. Those memories aren't just stored files in your mental archive—they're living, breathing experiences that your neural courthouse from Chapter 2 references every time you face relationship uncertainty.

The Science of Memory Healing:

- The reconsolidation window: Memories become changeable for approximately six hours after being recalled, creating opportunities to update them with new emotional information
- Somatic re-experiencing: The body holds attachment memories that cognitive approaches alone cannot reach—healing often requires feeling old emotions in a new, safe context
- Corrective emotional experiences: New positive experiences that directly contradict old attachment injuries can literally rewrite the emotional charge of traumatic memories

This isn't about erasing your past or pretending painful experiences didn't happen. It's about updating the emotional meaning your brain assigns to those experiences.

Marcus carried a visceral memory of his father leaving when he was seven—the sound of the door closing, the smell of his mother's tears, the crushing certainty that love always ends in abandonment. Traditional talk therapy helped him understand this pattern intellectually, but his body still braced for abandonment in every relationship.

His breakthrough came during a therapy session where he accessed this childhood memory while his therapist provided the steady, caring presence he'd never received. As the old memory surfaced with its familiar terror, he simultaneously experienced unconditional acceptance and safety. His nervous system began to update the original memory with new information: "I am worthy of staying. Love doesn't always leave."

This single session shifted a pattern that had controlled his relationships for thirty years.

The Body Remembers

Your amygdala doesn't speak in words—it speaks in sensations, images, and gut feelings. This is why purely cognitive approaches to healing often fall short. Your body holds the blueprint of your attachment patterns, and lasting change requires engaging both mind and nervous system.

The drama addiction we discussed earlier often stems from these unhealed attachment memories seeking resolution. Your brain keeps recreating familiar scenarios, hoping this time the story will end differently.

In Chapter 3, we'll see how these neural patterns and memory traces play out in your digital communications, where every delayed response can trigger decades-old abandonment fears.

3
THE TEXT MESSAGE TRIBUNAL - DECODING YOUR DIGITAL DESPERATION

WHEN BLUE CHECKMARKS BREED DIGITAL ANXIETY

The "seen" notification transforms from a simple read confirmation into evidence of rejection, activating deep-seated fears that someone has evaluated your worth and found you lacking. This digital anxiety stems from our primitive need for social acceptance, where being ignored once meant potential exile from the tribe. As we explored in the previous chapter, your amygdala cannot distinguish between modern digital silence and ancient threats to survival.

Your brain treats that blue checkmark like a courtroom verdict.

The catastrophic thinking spiral follows a predictable pattern: "Seen" becomes "They hate me" within minutes. Your mind races through worst-case scenarios, constructing elaborate stories about why someone hasn't responded. The physical anxiety symptoms triggered by digital silence mirror those of real danger - racing heart, sweaty palms, compulsive phone checking every few minutes.

Common Digital Anxiety Triggers:

- Read receipts without immediate responses
- Delayed replies to important messages
- Changes in texting patterns or frequency
- Social media activity without message responses
- Shorter responses than usual

The false urgency created by instant communication expectations compounds this anxiety. We expect immediate responses because technology makes them possible, forgetting that people have lives beyond their phones. Your anxious attachment system interprets normal delays as personal rejection.

Linda stared at her phone screen, the small "Read" notification under her message feeling like a verdict from a jury. She had sent a simple "How was your day?" to her new romantic interest three hours ago. Her mind began constructing elaborate scenarios: he was showing the message to friends and laughing, he was crafting a rejection text, or worse—he was already losing interest.

The rational part of her brain knew he could be in a meeting, driving, or simply busy. But the anxious part had already convicted him of emotional abandonment. By the time he responded two hours later with a warm, lengthy message about his hectic workday, she had mentally ended their relationship twice and composed three different "casual" follow-up messages she never sent.

This digital anxiety creates what we'll explore next in Chapter 4: the Fear Factory. Your mind manufactures abandonment scenarios where none exist, turning normal communication gaps into evidence of rejection.

NOW VS LATER BATTLE LINES

The internal battle between authentic communication and strategic game-playing creates exhausting mental gymnastics where every response time becomes a calculated move rather than natural interaction. This transforms genuine connection into a chess match where vulnerability becomes a tactical disadvantage. As we learned from the neuroscience courtroom in Chapter 2, your brain is already working overtime processing attachment signals - adding strategic timing calculations creates even more cognitive burden.

Your mind becomes a battlefield between now and later.

The "three-hour rule" and other arbitrary timing strategies prioritize appearing unavailable over authentic connection. These unwritten rules suggest that immediate responses signal desperation, while delayed responses demonstrate value and desirability. But these strategies backfire spectacularly for anxious attachment styles, creating the very distance and uncertainty that triggers your deepest fears.

Common Timing Battle Strategies:

- Waiting specific time periods before responding
- Matching or exceeding the other person's response delay
- Never being the first to text good morning
- Calculating "acceptable" response windows for different relationship stages
- Using read receipts as strategic weapons

How immediate responses get labeled as "desperate" while delayed responses create anxiety and distance reveals the impossible double bind of modern dating. You want to respond authentically, but fear being judged as too eager. You delay responses to appear "cool," but the waiting creates anxiety for both parties involved.

The energy drain of constantly calculating optimal response timing instead of focusing on message content steals attention from what actually matters - the quality of your communication and connection. You spend mental resources on performance rather than presence.

Lucas found himself in a ridiculous routine: receiving a text, typing an immediate response, then setting a timer for exactly forty-seven minutes before sending it. His friends had convinced him that responding too quickly made him look "thirsty," so he developed an elaborate system of delayed responses. He would screenshot conversations to analyze response times, trying to match or slightly exceed the other person's delay.

The irony wasn't lost on him that he was spending more mental energy on when to respond than on what to say. When Helen finally told him she appreciated his thoughtful, quick responses early in their relationship and found his later delays confusing and distant, he realized he had been playing a game no one else knew existed.

This exhausting internal battle sets the stage for Chapter 4, where we'll explore how your mind manufactures abandonment scenarios from these normal communication patterns.

HIDDEN MESSAGES MEET DIGITAL MINDS

Digital communication strips away 93% of human communication cues, leaving anxious minds to fill the void with worst-case scenarios. Without tone, body language, and facial expressions, simple messages become cryptographic puzzles requiring extensive analysis and interpretation. Your brain, already hypervigilant for attachment threats as we discussed in Chapter 2, goes into overdrive trying to decode meaning from limited digital signals.

Text becomes a mystery your mind desperately needs to solve.

Analyzing punctuation patterns becomes a specialized skill for anxious attachment styles. Periods transform into signs of aggression, while lack of exclamation points signals disinterest. Question marks can feel accusatory, and emoji choices carry enormous emotional weight. Your mind assigns meaning to every digital choice, creating elaborate interpretations from simple formatting decisions.

Digital Detective Clues:

- Period placement and frequency changes
- Emoji usage patterns and variations
- Response length compared to previous messages
- Capitalization shifts and formatting differences
- Time stamps and read receipt timing

The dangerous game of comparing current message tone to previous conversations creates false evidence of changing feelings. You become a digital archaeologist, excavating old conversations for baseline comparisons. A shorter response today means declining interest. Different word choices indicate emotional distance. Your mind builds cases from circumstantial evidence.

How asking for clarification becomes scarier than living with uncertainty reveals the core anxious attachment dilemma. You would rather suffer in ambiguous interpretation than risk confirming your worst fears through direct communication. The possibility of misunderstanding feels safer than the potential reality of actual disinterest.

Rebecca had developed a forensic approach to text analysis that would impress criminal investigators. When her partner responded "okay" instead of "okay!" she spent twenty minutes analyzing their previous messages to determine if this represented a shift in enthusiasm. She created mental databases: periods meant anger, lowercase meant disinterest, delayed responses meant loss of attraction.

She would screenshot conversations to friends for "expert analysis," turning every interaction into a group interpretation project. The breaking point came when she confronted her partner about being "short" with her, only to discover he had been in back-to-back meetings and was actually impressed by her patience.

Her elaborate detective work had been solving crimes that never existed.

This pattern of manufacturing meaning from minimal cues sets the foundation for Chapter 4, where we'll explore how your mind creates entire abandonment scenarios from these misinterpreted digital signals.

WHEN SCREENS STAND BETWEEN HEARTS

The smartphone paradox reveals devices designed to connect us can become shields that prevent real intimacy, allowing us to control our availability and emotional exposure while simultaneously creating new forms of relationship anxiety and distance. Your phone becomes both bridge and barrier, connecting you digitally while potentially isolating you emotionally.

Technology promises connection but often delivers performance instead.

The false sense of connection through constant digital contact can replace deeper, more vulnerable in-person interactions. You might text all day but struggle with eye contact during dinner. Emoji conversations feel safer than reading facial expressions. Your digital intimacy soars while your physical presence becomes awkward and stilted.

How digital communication allows for emotional editing and presentation management inhibits authentic self-expression. You can craft the perfect response, delete and retype messages, and present your most polished self. This editing capability, while reducing immediate vulnerability, prevents partners from knowing your unfiltered thoughts and genuine reactions.

Digital Distance Indicators:

- Preferring text conversations over phone calls
- Feeling more articulate in writing than in person
- Using phones during face-to-face time together
- Seeking validation through digital metrics over partner feedback
- Avoiding difficult conversations until you can "script" them

The addiction to digital validation through likes, responses, and read receipts can overshadow genuine relationship satisfaction. You chase notification dopamine while your actual relationship needs remain unmet. The constant availability of digital feedback creates unrealistic expectations for immediate validation in all interactions.

David realized his relationship was being conducted entirely through screens when he and his girlfriend spent an entire evening together, both responding to each other's Instagram stories instead of talking. They had become more comfortable expressing feelings through carefully crafted texts than spontaneous face-to-face conversations. He could write paragraphs about his emotions via message but struggled to maintain eye contact during serious discussions.

Their digital intimacy was high—constant texting, sharing memes, long voice messages—but their physical presence felt awkward and stilted. The phone had become a security blanket that allowed them to connect while maintaining emotional distance, creating an illusion of closeness that crumbled during unmediated interactions.

As we transition into Chapter 4, we'll explore how the same pattern-matching anxiety that drives your digital detective work manifests in face-to-face interactions, where your mind manufactures abandonment scenarios from normal social cues and everyday relationship fluctuations.

4
THE FEAR FACTORY - MANUFACTURING ABANDONMENT WHERE NONE EXISTS

WHEN PREDICTIONS SHAPE THEIR OWN DESTINY

Diana stared at her phone, analyzing every word of her boyfriend's text: "Hey, running late tonight. Might have to reschedule dinner." Her mind immediately jumped to conclusions—he was losing interest, pulling away, probably meeting someone else. She fired back a passive-aggressive response about how he "obviously had better things to do." When he finally called hours later, confused and hurt by her reaction, their conversation turned into an argument that left both feeling disconnected. What started as a simple scheduling conflict became the relationship crisis she had predicted.

The prediction paradox reveals how our fear-based assumptions can create the very outcomes we're trying to avoid. When we operate from a place of anticipated abandonment, we often behave in ways that push people away, then use their withdrawal as evidence that our fears were justified. This creates a vicious cycle where our protective mechanisms become the source of our pain.

Remember how we explored digital desperation in the previous chapter? Those same anxious patterns of overanalyzing texts extend into a broader tendency to manufacture abandonment scenarios. Your brain, already primed for threat detection from those early attachment experiences we uncovered in Chapter 1, becomes a prediction machine running worst-case scenarios on repeat.

The self-fulfilling prophecy works through several mechanisms:

- Confirmation bias in action: We selectively notice evidence that supports our fears while dismissing contradictory information
- Behavioral contamination: Our anxious energy and defensive responses influence how others interact with us
- Reality distortion: We interpret neutral or positive signals through a lens of impending doom

Elliott had always prided himself on being intuitive about relationships, but his track record told a different story. Every relationship ended the same way—with him becoming increasingly suspicious and controlling as he sensed his partner "pulling away." He would interrogate his girlfriends about their whereabouts, analyze their tone of voice for signs of disinterest, and create tests to gauge their commitment. Without fail, his partners would eventually become exhausted by his constant need for reassurance and end the relationship.

He saw this as proof of his accurate intuition.

Elliott never recognized that his behavior was manufacturing the abandonment he feared most. This pattern will become even clearer as we explore intimacy struggles in the next chapter.

WHEN YOUR GUARD DOG TURNS ROGUE

Hypervigilance feels like a superpower when you're scanning for threats—until you realize you're living in a state of constant alarm that exhausts both you and everyone around you. What begins as an adaptive response to protect against abandonment transforms into a relationship saboteur that creates the very distance you're trying to prevent.

This heightened state of awareness stems from your brain's threat detection system that we explored in Chapter 2. Your amygdala, already primed from early attachment wounds, becomes oversensitive to any signal that could indicate rejection or abandonment. Like a smoke detector that goes off when you burn toast, your internal alarm system starts responding to normal relationship fluctuations as if they were five-alarm fires.

The hypervigilant mind operates through several destructive mechanisms:

- The energy drain: Constant monitoring depletes your mental resources and makes genuine presence impossible
- False alarms: Hypervigilance generates numerous threat alerts that turn out to be misinterpretations, training you to distrust your own perceptions
- Intimacy interference: Partners feel like they're under surveillance rather than in a loving relationship

Dorothy described her dating life as "being a detective in my own relationship." She monitored her partner's social media activity, noticed changes in his texting patterns, and kept mental notes about his moods and behaviors. She could tell you exactly how many times he'd said "I love you" that week compared to the week before, and she had theories about what each variation meant.

Her hypervigilance felt protective—she was staying ahead of potential problems.

But her partner began to feel suffocated by her intense focus on every micro-expression and interaction. He started withdrawing not because he loved her less, but because he felt like he couldn't breathe or be human without it being analyzed for signs of relationship decline.

Remember those text message spirals from Chapter 3? Hypervigilance is the broader pattern behind that digital desperation. You're not just overthinking messages—you're overthinking everything. Every delayed response, every slight change in tone, every moment when your partner seems distracted becomes potential evidence of impending abandonment.

This constant state of alert prevents the very intimacy you crave, setting the stage for the closeness paradoxes we'll explore in the next chapter.

WHEN YOUR MIND SOUNDS FALSE ALARMS

Your rejection sensitivity acts like an overzealous jury, finding guilt in every neutral expression and interpreting evidence through the lens of predetermined conclusions. While sensitivity to social cues can be valuable, rejection sensitivity operates with such a low threshold for "evidence" that it convicts innocent interactions and sentences you to emotional turmoil based on circumstantial evidence.

This hypersensitive alert system connects directly to the neural pathways we examined in Chapter 2. Your brain's threat detection center, already wired for maximum protection from those early attachment experiences, processes ambiguous social signals as clear danger. What should be simple daily interactions become complex trials where you're always waiting for the verdict of rejection.

The rejection sensitivity jury operates through predictable distortions:

- Threshold distortion: Normal relationship fluctuations get classified as rejection signals
- Projection patterns: You attribute your own fears and insecurities to others' motivations and behaviors
- Evidence manufacturing: Ambiguous situations get filled in with worst-case scenario assumptions

Marcus could read rejection into almost any interaction. When his girlfriend took longer than usual to text back, he saw disinterest. When she seemed tired after work, he interpreted it as emotional withdrawal from him. When she wanted to spend time with friends, he felt pushed aside and unimportant.

His rejection sensitivity jury was always in session, deliberating over every piece of "evidence" and consistently returning guilty verdicts.

The irony was that his girlfriend was actually quite content in the relationship—until his constant need for reassurance and his defensive reactions to her normal human behaviors began to create actual distance between them. His sensitivity, designed to protect him from rejection, became the very mechanism that manufactured it.

This pattern builds on the digital desperation we explored in Chapter 3, but extends far beyond text messages. You're not just misreading delayed responses—you're misreading facial expressions, tone of voice, body language, and social dynamics. Every interaction becomes a potential source of evidence for your prosecution case against yourself.

The rejection sensitivity jury never seems to consider alternative explanations. Your partner isn't tired from work—they're growing distant. Your friend isn't busy—they're losing interest. Your date isn't nervous—they're already planning their escape.

This constant state of expecting rejection creates the perfect conditions for the intimacy struggles we'll examine next, where getting close feels inherently dangerous.

WHEN PREPARATION BECOMES MENTAL TORTURE

Catastrophic thinking masquerades as preparation, convincing you that imagining worst-case scenarios will somehow protect you from them. But this mental court session, where you prosecute every possible negative outcome, becomes a torture device that subjects you to emotional pain for events that may never occur.

This pattern connects to the neural threat detection we explored in Chapter 2, where your brain's survival circuits become overactive. Your amygdala treats imagined future scenarios as present dangers, flooding your system with stress hormones and creating genuine emotional distress over fictional events.

The catastrophic thinking trap operates through several destructive mechanisms:

- Mental rehearsal trap: Repeatedly imagining abandonment scenarios creates neural pathways that make these outcomes feel more likely and inevitable
- Present moment theft: Catastrophic thinking pulls you out of current relationship satisfaction and into imaginary future disasters
- Emotional exhaustion: You experience the pain of loss and rejection repeatedly, even when your relationship is stable

Sarah spent hours each day in what she called "worst-case scenario planning." She would imagine her boyfriend leaving her, picture how the breakup conversation would go, and mentally prepare her responses to various rejection scenarios. She told herself this was smart preparation—if something bad happened, she'd be ready.

But this mental rehearsal was stealing her ability to enjoy the relationship she actually had.

She was experiencing breakup grief while still in a committed relationship, and her emotional distance created by this catastrophic thinking began to concern her boyfriend, who couldn't understand why she seemed sad and disconnected even during their happiest moments together.

Like the text message spirals from Chapter 3, catastrophic thinking creates suffering where none previously existed. You're not just overthinking digital communication—you're overthinking every possible future scenario until you've emotionally lived through dozens of breakups that haven't happened.

This mental torture chamber convinces you that preparation equals protection, but it actually weakens your ability to handle real challenges by depleting your emotional resources on imaginary problems. When actual relationship issues arise, you're already emotionally exhausted from fighting battles that existed only in your mind.

The fear factory we've explored throughout this chapter—from prediction paradoxes to rejection sensitivity—all feeds into this catastrophic thinking pattern. Your mind becomes a generator of abandonment scenarios, manufacturing emotional pain as efficiently as any external threat could.

Understanding these patterns prepares us for examining how intimacy itself becomes threatening when filtered through anxious attachment.

5
THE INTIMACY INQUISITION - WHY GETTING CLOSE FEELS LIKE GETTING BURNED

WHEN WALLS COME DOWN

The vulnerability paradox sits at the heart of anxious attachment's most confusing contradiction: we desperately crave emotional intimacy, yet every attempt to be vulnerable feels like handing someone a loaded weapon. This internal conflict creates a maddening cycle where the very thing that could heal our relationships becomes the source of our greatest terror.

Remember the abandonment fears we explored in Chapter 4? They transform vulnerability into a high-stakes gamble rather than a natural relationship process.

The Three Faces of Intimacy Self-Sabotage:

- Over-disclosure as armor: Anxiously attached individuals often mistake emotional dumping for vulnerability, sharing too much too soon as a way to test whether someone will stay or flee

- The authenticity trap: Believing that being "real" means sharing every insecurity, fear, and need without consideration for timing, context, or the other person's capacity
- Vulnerability timing dysfunction: Either shutting down completely or opening the floodgates at inappropriate moments, creating emotional whiplash in relationships

Penelope had been dating Ian for three weeks when she decided it was time to "be vulnerable." During what he thought was a casual dinner, she launched into a detailed account of her childhood abandonment fears, her previous relationship traumas, and her desperate need for reassurance about their future together. She interpreted his overwhelmed silence as rejection and began crying, asking if he was going to leave her like everyone else.

What she thought was brave openness actually pushed him away.

Not because he couldn't handle her emotions, but because the intensity felt manipulative rather than genuine. Her vulnerability had become a weapon to extract promises rather than a bridge to deeper connection.

Your brain's threat detection system, which we examined in Chapter 2, treats intimacy like a courtroom where you're always on trial. Every shared feeling becomes evidence that could be used against you. This creates what psychologists call "intimacy anorexia" - starving yourself of the very connection you crave because the risk feels unbearable.

The cruel irony? True vulnerability requires the secure base that anxious attachment makes nearly impossible to create. You end up performing vulnerability rather than living it, which explains why your attempts at closeness often backfire spectacularly.

This pattern sets up our next exploration: how the drive to be "nice" becomes another prison, keeping you from the authentic connections you desperately seek.

WHEN LOVE BECOMES A CAGE

Emotional fusion occurs when anxiously attached individuals lose themselves so completely in their relationships that they can no longer distinguish their emotions, needs, and identity from their partner's. What begins as deep connection transforms into suffocating enmeshment that destroys the very intimacy they sought to create.

This builds directly on the abandonment fears we explored in Chapter 4, where the terror of being left alone drives you to merge completely with another person. Your brain's threat detection system, which we examined in Chapter 2, interprets any separateness as dangerous.

The Three Stages of Emotional Fusion:

- Emotional contagion syndrome: Absorbing your partner's moods, stress, and problems as if they were your own, leading to constant emotional turbulence and the inability to maintain your own emotional equilibrium
- Identity dissolution: Gradually abandoning your interests, friendships, and goals to become whatever you think your partner wants, ultimately becoming so shapeless that there's nothing left for them to love
- The merger fantasy: Believing that true love means becoming "one person" rather than two whole individuals choosing to share their lives together

Finn noticed the shift happening gradually with his girlfriend. At first, he appreciated how interested she seemed in his hobbies—

joining his rock climbing group, reading the books he recommended, even changing her music preferences to match his. But six months in, he realized she had completely abandoned her own interests. When he asked what she wanted to do for her birthday, she couldn't answer.

When he suggested she spend time with her old friends, she panicked, asking if he was trying to get rid of her.

The woman he had fallen for—vibrant, opinionated, passionate about her art—had disappeared entirely. In trying to become everything he wanted, she had become nothing at all.

This emotional fusion creates what psychologists call "undifferentiation"—the inability to maintain your sense of self while in close relationship with others. You become so afraid of conflict or disapproval that you preemptively erase yourself, thinking this will guarantee love and prevent abandonment.

The tragic irony? Partners often fall in love with your authentic self, then watch in confusion as that person gradually vanishes. The very strategy meant to secure love actually repels it, because healthy people are attracted to whole individuals, not emotional chameleons.

This fusion dynamic perfectly sets up our next exploration: how the compulsive need to be "nice" becomes another form of self-erasure, trapping you in patterns that prevent genuine intimacy.

WHEN HEARTS MEET CALCULATED MINDS

Anxiously attached individuals often struggle with a false dichotomy between being "authentic" and being "strategic" in relationships, believing that any form of emotional regulation or thoughtful communication is manipulation. This black-and-white thinking prevents them from developing the nuanced social skills necessary for healthy intimacy.

This connects directly to the abandonment fears we explored in Chapter 4, where the terror of being "found out" as fake drives you toward extreme emotional transparency. Your brain's threat detection system, examined in Chapter 2, treats any emotional filtering as dangerous deception.

The Three Faces of Misguided Authenticity:

- The emotional vomit phenomenon: Confusing authenticity with unfiltered emotional expression, believing that healthy relationships require sharing every fleeting thought and feeling without consideration for impact or timing
- Strategic communication as betrayal: Viewing any attempt to regulate emotions or choose words carefully as "fake" or manipulative, missing the reality that all successful relationships require emotional intelligence and social awareness
- The spontaneity trap: Believing that planned or thoughtful gestures are less meaningful than impulsive ones, leading to chaotic relationship dynamics driven by emotional reactivity rather than intentional love

Ivy prided herself on being "brutally honest" in relationships. When she felt insecure, she said so immediately. When she was angry, she expressed it without filter. When she needed reassurance, she demanded it on the spot. She viewed her boyfriend's suggestion that they "talk about this when we're both calmer" as him being inauthentic and emotionally unavailable.

But her "authenticity" was actually emotional tyranny.

She was forcing her partner to manage her unregulated emotions while labeling any request for consideration as fake. When he finally ended the relationship, she felt vindicated: "See? He couldn't handle the real me." In reality, he couldn't handle being her emotional dumping ground while being criticized for having any emotional needs of his own.

True authenticity isn't about emotional incontinence—it's about being genuinely yourself while considering the impact of your actions on others. Healthy relationships require both emotional honesty and emotional intelligence, both spontaneity and thoughtfulness.

The distinction matters because this confusion about authenticity feeds directly into another destructive pattern: the compulsive need to be perpetually "nice" at the expense of your own needs, which becomes its own form of emotional prison.

THE LOVE YOU PUSH AWAY

The intimacy thermostat is an unconscious regulatory system that kicks in when relationships become "too good," causing anxiously attached individuals to create chaos, pick fights, or withdraw just as they're getting the love they've always wanted. This self-sabotage mechanism operates from the belief that they don't deserve love and that disappointment is inevitable.

This connects to the abandonment fears we explored in Chapter 4, but with a cruel twist: instead of fearing abandonment, you create it. Your brain's threat detection system, examined in Chapter 2, treats genuine love as more dangerous than familiar pain.

The Three Stages of Love Sabotage:

- Success panic syndrome: Experiencing overwhelming anxiety when relationships are going maintaining the illusion of control while ensuring the feared abandonment actually occurs

Brett had never been happier in a relationship. His girlfriend was kind, consistent, and clearly loved him. But instead of feeling grateful, he felt terrified. He began picking fights over small things, testing her commitment by being increasingly demanding and critical. When she planned a surprise weekend getaway for his birthday, he accused her of being controlling and trying to change him.

He started flirting with other women and leaving his dating apps visible on his phone.

When she finally confronted him about his behavior, he felt a familiar rush of relief—this he could handle. The calm waters of a healthy relationship felt more dangerous than the familiar storms of dysfunction. By the time he realized what he had done, she was gone, and he was left with the painful recognition that he had destroyed the best thing in his life because he couldn't believe he deserved it.

This thermostat operates on a simple but devastating logic: if love is inevitable going to end in pain, better to control when and how that pain arrives. The problem is that this "protection" ensures you never experience the very thing you're desperately seeking.

Understanding these self-sabotage patterns prepares us for our next crucial exploration: how the compulsive need to be perpetually "nice" becomes another form of self-betrayal that prevents authentic intimacy.

6
THE PEOPLE-PLEASING PROSECUTION - WHEN NICE BECOMES A PRISON

WHEN NICE BECOMES A WEAPON

When Quinn started therapy, she described herself as "just a really caring person." She volunteered for every committee at work, never missed a friend's birthday, and always said yes to social invitations even when exhausted. But beneath her cheerful exterior, she was drowning in resentment and anxiety, constantly calculating what others needed from her to maintain their approval.

The distinction between genuine care and manipulative niceness lies in motivation and energy. Genuine care flows from abundance and choice—you give because you want to, not because you're terrified of what happens if you don't. Manipulative niceness, though often unconscious, operates from scarcity and fear, using kindness as currency to purchase acceptance and avoid rejection.

People-pleasers weaponize their niceness in subtle ways that even they don't recognize. They create debt systems where their kindness becomes leverage for future relationship security. When someone doesn't reciprocate their excessive giving, they feel betrayed and abandoned, not realizing they've been conducting an unconscious transaction rather than expressing authentic care.

The difference becomes clear in these key areas:

- Genuine care respects both your needs and others', while manipulative niceness sacrifices your well-being for others' comfort
- Authentic kindness can say no when necessary, while people-pleasing niceness feels compelled to say yes regardless of personal cost
- Real compassion includes self-compassion, while approval addiction treats self-care as selfish and dangerous

Isaac realized his "niceness" was actually manipulation when his girlfriend pointed out that his constant gifts and favors felt suffocating rather than loving. He had been trying to earn her affection rather than simply expressing it, creating an exhausting dynamic where both felt trapped—he in his performance, and she in her guilt over not appreciating his efforts enough.

This weaponized niceness stems directly from the intimacy fears we explored in Chapter 5. When getting close feels dangerous, we use excessive giving as a shield, hoping our indispensability will prevent abandonment. But this strategy backfires spectacularly.

Understanding this pattern prepares us for Chapter 7, where we'll examine how these people-pleasing tendencies influence our partner selection. The people we choose often reflect our unconscious beliefs about what we must do to be lovable.

THE SILENT PRICE OF PEACE

Sarah prided herself on never fighting with anyone. Her marriage appeared harmonious to outsiders, her friendships seemed effortless, and her workplace relationships were always pleasant. Yet she found herself lying awake at night, replaying conversations and building elaborate mental cases against people who had no idea she was upset with them.

True peace isn't the absence of conflict—it's the presence of honest communication and resolved tension. When we avoid all disagreement in the name of harmony, we create a false peace built on suppressed authentic feelings and unaddressed issues that eventually explode or implode.

The silent price of this artificial peace shows up in multiple ways:

- Conflict avoidance creates emotional debt that compounds over time, leading to sudden relationship explosions over seemingly minor issues
- Suppressed disagreements prevent genuine intimacy because real connection requires knowing and accepting each other's full truth
- Avoiding difficult conversations teaches others that your boundaries are negotiable and your feelings don't matter

Michael discovered that his conflict avoidance was actually creating more conflict when his business partnership nearly dissolved. Years of swallowing disagreements about company direction had built into a wall of resentment that made collaboration impossible. When he finally learned to address issues directly and kindly, their working relationship transformed from polite tension to genuine partnership.

This pattern connects directly to the intimacy fears we explored in Chapter 5. When closeness feels threatening, we unconsciously believe that any disagreement will lead to abandonment. So we sacrifice our authentic voice to maintain the illusion of connection, not realizing we're actually preventing real intimacy from developing.

The anxious attachment system, as we learned in Chapter 2, interprets conflict as existential threat. Your nervous system floods with panic at the first sign of tension, making it feel safer to retreat into people-pleasing silence than to risk expressing your true thoughts and feelings.

But here's what your anxious brain doesn't understand: relationships that can't handle disagreement can't handle intimacy either. The very conflicts you're avoiding are often the conversations that would deepen your connections and resolve the underlying issues creating distance.

This silent price of peace directly influences your partner selection, which we'll explore in Chapter 7. Understanding how conflict avoidance shapes your relationship choices reveals why you might unconsciously gravitate toward people who reinforce these patterns.

TWO FACES OF LOVE

Growing up in a household where emotional volatility meant danger, Charlotte learned to read every micro-expression and adjust her personality accordingly. With her analytical friends, she became more serious. With her adventurous sister, she forced enthusiasm for activities she disliked. With her critical mother, she became a perfectionist people-pleaser. But she had no idea who she actually was when no one was watching.

The adapted self is the version of you that developed to survive and gain acceptance in your early environment. While this adaptation served an important protective function, continuing to live primarily from this false self in adult relationships prevents genuine intimacy and creates exhausting internal pressure to maintain a performance.

This split creates two distinct faces of love—the love you receive for your adapted self, and the love that's possible for your authentic self. The adapted self receives conditional approval based on meeting others' expectations. The authentic self, though riskier to reveal, offers the possibility of unconditional acceptance.

The costs of living from your adapted self include:

- Constant monitoring of others' reactions and adjusting behavior to maintain approval, leading to chronic anxiety and emotional exhaustion
- Surface-level connections that prevent others from truly knowing and loving the real you, creating deep loneliness even in relationships
- Internal disconnection from your own needs, preferences, and feelings, making it impossible to advocate for yourself or experience genuine satisfaction

Daniel spent years being the "fun guy" in his friend group, always up for anything, never expressing preferences or needs. When depression hit and he couldn't maintain the performance, he expected his friendships to crumble. Instead, his closest friends expressed relief at finally meeting the real him and shared their own struggles with authenticity. His vulnerability deepened rather than destroyed his relationships.

This pattern connects to the intimacy fears from Chapter 5—we develop these adaptive personas precisely because authentic intimacy feels dangerous. The people-pleasing strategies we've explored become the tools our adapted self uses to maintain safety and approval.

Understanding these two faces of love becomes crucial as we move into Chapter 7, where we'll examine how your adapted self influences partner selection. The relationships you choose often reflect which version of yourself you believe is most lovable.

WHEN GIVING ALWAYS TAKES EVERYTHING

Melissa couldn't understand why she felt so angry all the time when everyone in her life seemed happy with her. She was the friend everyone called for favors, the employee who stayed late without complaint, the daughter who never caused problems. But inside, she was keeping score of every sacrifice, building a case for how much she gave and how little she received, even though she never asked for anything in return.

Resentment is the inevitable result of consistently abandoning yourself for others' comfort. When you say yes with your mouth but no with your heart, when you give without genuine willingness, when you accommodate others while ignoring your own needs, you create an internal ledger of unpaid debts that poisons your relationships and your peace of mind.

This toxic cycle manifests in predictable ways:

- Constant accommodation without reciprocity creates a victim mentality where you feel perpetually taken advantage of, even when others have no idea you're sacrificing
- Suppressed resentment leaks out through passive-aggressive behavior, emotional withdrawal, and sudden explosive anger over minor issues
- The resentment cycle perpetuates itself: the more you accommodate without boundaries, the more others expect accommodation, leading to increased pressure and anger

Kevin finally understood his pattern when his wife asked why he seemed so angry after hosting his family for the holidays. He had spent weeks preparing, accommodating everyone's dietary restrictions and preferences, never expressing his own needs or limits. His "generous" hosting had actually been a setup for resentment, as he expected appreciation and recognition that never came because no one knew he was sacrificing.

Learning to host authentically—with clear boundaries and shared responsibilities—transformed family gatherings from resentful obligations into genuine celebrations.

This connects directly to our exploration of intimacy fears in Chapter 5. When closeness feels dangerous, we use excessive giving as protection, believing our indispensability prevents abandonment. But this strategy backfires, creating the very resentment and distance we feared.

The people-pleasing patterns we've examined throughout this chapter—weaponizing niceness, avoiding conflict, living from our adapted self, and giving until resentment builds—all stem from the same core belief: authentic connection is too risky.

Understanding these dynamics prepares us for Chapter 7, where we'll explore how these people-pleasing tendencies unconsciously influence our partner selection, often drawing us toward people who reinforce rather than heal these exhausting patterns.

7
THE PARTNER SELECTION PANEL - WHY YOU CHOOSE WHO YOU CHOOSE

WHEN HEARTS CRAVE FAMILIAR PAIN

The truth is, we don't choose partners randomly. Deep within our psyche operates what I call the "Partner Selection Panel"—a complex internal system that evaluates potential mates based on our attachment patterns, unhealed wounds, and unconscious beliefs about love. Understanding this system is crucial to breaking free from the exhausting cycle of overthinking every interaction and finally gaining the emotional peace you've been seeking.

The Familiar vs. The Healthy: Attraction to Emotional Unavailability

Your nervous system has been trained to recognize "love" through specific emotional signatures—often ones that mirror your earliest attachment experiences. When someone treats you with consistent kindness and availability, your system may interpret this as "boring" or "not real love" because it lacks the familiar activation patterns of anxiety and uncertainty.

This connects directly to the people-pleasing patterns we explored in Chapter 6. When you're used to working hard for scraps of attention, freely given love feels suspicious.

Your brain doesn't distinguish between familiar and healthy.

- Familiarity breeds attraction, not necessarily health: Your brain interprets familiar relationship dynamics as "home," even when home was chaotic or painful
- The unavailable partner paradox: Emotionally unavailable partners trigger the same neural pathways that were activated in childhood when seeking attention from inconsistent caregivers
- Secure attachment feels "flat": Without the chemical highs and lows of anxious attachment, secure relationships can initially feel less intense or exciting

Evan had a pattern of falling for women who were "mysterious" and hard to read. His last three relationships followed the same script: intense initial attraction to someone who seemed interested but distant, months of trying to "win" her over, brief periods of connection followed by withdrawal, and eventual heartbreak. When his friend introduced him to Catherine, a warm, communicative woman who showed genuine interest in him, his first thought was, "She's nice, but there's no spark."

It took months of therapy for him to realize that his definition of "spark" was actually anxiety.

The absence of that familiar tension didn't mean the absence of genuine connection—it meant the presence of safety. This revelation would become the foundation for the healing experiments we'll explore in Chapter 8, where you'll learn to rewire your attraction patterns and embrace the unfamiliar comfort of secure love.

SAVING OTHERS WHILE RUNNING FROM YOURSELF

Many people with anxious attachment are drawn to partners who need "fixing" because it provides a sense of purpose and control in the relationship. If you can heal them, the logic goes, they'll never leave you. This dynamic allows you to focus on someone else's problems rather than confronting your own patterns of insecurity and abandonment fears.

This connects directly to the people-pleasing patterns we explored in Chapter 6, where being "needed" becomes your primary strategy for securing love. The rescuer complex takes this one step further—turning relationships into rehabilitation projects.

Your Partner Selection Panel actively scans for wounded birds to nurse back to health.

- The fixer's high: Helping others releases dopamine and creates a sense of being needed, which temporarily soothes abandonment anxiety
- Control through caretaking: When you're focused on healing someone else, you feel like you have agency in the relationship's outcome
- Avoiding your own healing: Rescuing others becomes a sophisticated form of self-avoidance, keeping you distracted from your own growth work
- The gratitude trap: You believe that if someone owes you their recovery, they'll be obligated to stay

Ava realized she had a type: brilliant, creative men with "potential" who were struggling with addiction, depression, or commitment issues. She would enter each relationship believing that her love could heal them, spending months or years trying to be the perfect supportive partner. The pattern always ended the same way—with her exhausted and them moving on to someone else, often displaying the very emotional availability with their new partner that they'd never shown her.

In therapy, she discovered that her rescuer complex allowed her to avoid confronting her own deep-seated belief that she wasn't worthy of love unless she was useful. By staying busy fixing others, she never had to sit with her own emotional needs or examine why she felt so empty when she wasn't actively helping someone.

The cruel irony is obvious: while you're trying to heal others to prevent abandonment, you're actually choosing people who are least equipped to provide the security you crave.

This pattern keeps you stuck in the very anxiety you're trying to escape. In Chapter 8, we'll explore how to redirect this healing energy inward, learning to become your own primary caretaker instead of constantly seeking validation through others' recovery.

WHEN STABILITY FEELS LIKE SETTLING

When you're accustomed to the emotional rollercoaster of anxious attachment, secure partners can initially feel underwhelming. They don't trigger your fight-or-flight system, they don't create dramatic highs and lows, and they don't activate your hypervigilant scanning for signs of abandonment. This can be misinterpreted as a lack of chemistry when it's actually the presence of safety.

Remember the people-pleasing patterns from Chapter 6? When someone doesn't require constant effort to maintain their interest, your nervous system doesn't know what to do with itself. The absence of anxiety feels foreign, even boring.

Your Partner Selection Panel has been programmed to equate intensity with intimacy.

- Mistaking anxiety for attraction: The adrenaline and cortisol released during relationship uncertainty can feel like passion and excitement
- The addiction to emotional intensity: Anxious attachment creates neurochemical patterns similar to addiction, making calm relationships feel "flat" by comparison
- Redefining chemistry: True chemistry includes safety, trust, and the ability to be authentic without fear of abandonment
- The withdrawal effect: When drama is removed, your system experiences something akin to withdrawal, making you crave the familiar chaos

Andrew described his relationship with his current partner this way: "The first few months, I kept waiting for the other shoe to drop. She was consistent, she communicated clearly, and she seemed genuinely happy to be with me. I actually broke up with her twice because I convinced myself we didn't have enough 'passion.' Each time, I'd go back to dating women who kept me guessing, and I'd remember why I was so miserable."

It took him almost a year to understand that the "boring" feeling he had with her was actually peace. His nervous system was finally calm enough to actually connect instead of just react.

This is where the real work begins. Stability isn't settling—it's the foundation for genuine intimacy. When you're not constantly managing relationship crises, you have energy available for deeper connection, personal growth, and authentic self-expression.

The healing experiments we'll explore in Chapter 8 will help you retrain your nervous system to recognize safety as desirable rather than suspicious. You'll learn to distinguish between the excitement of uncertainty and the joy of secure connection.

WHEN BUTTERFLIES LIE TO YOU

What many people mistake for "chemistry" is actually their nervous system responding to familiar patterns of activation. The butterflies, the obsessive thoughts, the inability to eat or sleep—these aren't signs of true love, they're signs of an activated attachment system responding to uncertainty and potential threat.

This connects to everything we've explored: the people-pleasing from Chapter 6, the digital desperation from Chapter 3, and the fear factory from Chapter 4. Your body has learned to interpret stress as passion.

Real chemistry doesn't require suffering to feel intense.

- Trauma bonding vs. genuine bonding: Intense emotional experiences, even negative ones, create powerful neurochemical bonds that can be mistaken for deep connection
- The uncertainty addiction: Intermittent reinforcement (unpredictable responses from partners) creates stronger psychological bonds than consistent positive reinforcement
- Recognizing true chemistry: Authentic attraction includes feeling seen, understood, and safe to be vulnerable
- The stress-passion confusion: Your body releases the same chemicals during relationship anxiety as it does during excitement

Rosa kept a journal during her last relationship, documenting her emotional states. Looking back, she noticed a clear pattern: her most "passionate" days coincided with her partner being distant or critical, while the days when he was loving and present barely registered in her memory. "I was literally addicted to the feeling of almost losing him," she realized. "The relief when he'd be sweet again felt like love, but it was just my nervous system coming down from high alert."

Real love, she's learning, doesn't require that kind of suffering to feel intense.

Understanding Your Selection Patterns

Your partner selection isn't random—it's driven by deeply ingrained patterns designed to recreate familiar relationship dynamics, even when those dynamics cause pain. The familiar masquerades as attraction, leading you to choose emotionally unavailable partners who activate your anxiety rather than soothe it.

The rescuer complex allows you to focus on fixing others instead of healing yourself, while secure partners initially feel "boring" because they don't trigger your hypervigilant attachment system.

Understanding why you choose who you choose is only the first step. Once you recognize these patterns, the real work begins: learning how to rewire your attraction system in Chapter 8, where we'll transform these insights into practical healing experiments.

8

THE HEALING LABORATORY - EXPERIMENTING WITH NEW WAYS OF BEING

ALICE'S HEALING LABORATORY BEGINS

Remember Diana from Chapter 7, who kept choosing emotionally unavailable partners? Her healing journey began when she finally understood that her partner selection wasn't random bad luck. It was her attachment system desperately trying to recreate familiar dynamics.

Now comes the experimental phase.

Therapy Modalities on Trial: Finding Your Therapeutic Match

The world of trauma therapy offers multiple pathways to healing, each targeting different aspects of attachment wounds. While some modalities focus on rewiring thought patterns, others work directly with stored trauma in the body or help process traumatic memories through bilateral stimulation.

- EMDR (Eye Movement Desensitization and Reprocessing): Uses bilateral stimulation to help process traumatic memories and reduce their emotional charge, particularly effective for specific attachment traumas

- Cognitive Behavioral Therapy (CBT): Focuses on identifying and changing negative thought patterns and behaviors that stem from insecure attachment, helping break the cycle of overthinking interactions
- Somatic Approaches: Work directly with the body's stored trauma responses, helping regulate the nervous system and build capacity for genuine intimacy without overwhelming activation

George spent two years in traditional talk therapy analyzing his anxious attachment patterns, but his body still went into panic mode every time his partner seemed distant. When he switched to somatic experiencing therapy, he learned to recognize the physical sensations that preceded his clingy behaviors.

"For the first time, I could feel the anxiety rising in my chest and actually do something about it before I started sending desperate texts," he explained.

Within six months of body-based work, his relationships began shifting from desperate to secure as he developed the capacity to self-regulate his nervous system responses.

Diana discovered Internal Family Systems therapy helped her understand the different parts of herself that showed up in relationships. The part that desperately needed reassurance. The part that pushed people away when they got too close. The part that analyzed every interaction for signs of rejection.

"I stopped fighting against these parts and started getting curious about what they needed," she shared. "That curiosity changed everything."

The key is finding the therapeutic approach that resonates with your specific healing needs and nervous system responses.

THE MODERN HEALING DIVIDE**

The question of whether to use psychiatric medications as part of attachment healing creates intense internal conflict for many. This decision involves weighing the potential benefits of chemical support for anxiety and depression against concerns about masking symptoms or becoming dependent on external solutions.

Understanding your options helps make informed decisions:

- Medication as stabilization: Anti-anxiety medications or antidepressants can provide enough nervous system stability to engage effectively in therapy and practice new relational skills
- Natural regulation approaches: Techniques like breathwork, meditation, exercise, and nutritional support can help regulate mood and anxiety without pharmaceutical intervention
- Combination approaches: Many find success using short-term medication support while building long-term natural regulation skills, then gradually transitioning off medications

Ivy struggled with this decision for months, fearing that taking anxiety medication meant she was "weak" or "broken." Her over-thinking about every relationship interaction had become so severe that she couldn't sleep or focus at work. After three months on a low-dose anti-anxiety medication, she found herself able to pause before sending panicked texts to her partner and actually absorb what she was learning in therapy.

"The medication didn't fix my attachment issues," she reflected, "but it gave me enough space between my triggers and my reactions to start building new patterns. I was able to move from desperate and clingy to actually working on becoming secure."

Ethan chose a different path entirely. After experiencing side effects from antidepressants, he committed to natural approaches. He developed a morning routine of breathwork and meditation, changed his diet to reduce inflammation, and practiced yoga three times weekly. His progress took longer, but he felt more connected to his healing process.

"I needed to feel every step of getting better," he explained. "The slow approach taught me to trust my body's ability to regulate itself."

Neither approach is superior.

The goal remains the same regardless of your chosen path: developing the capacity to stay present with difficult emotions without being overwhelmed by them. Some people need pharmaceutical support to reach that capacity. Others find their way through natural methods.

What matters is choosing an approach that aligns with your values, circumstances, and nervous system needs. The 90-day practice program in Chapter 9 works effectively with or without medication support, adapting to whatever foundation you're building from.

GOING SOLO OR FINDING YOUR GUIDE

The abundance of attachment-focused books, podcasts, and online resources creates the appealing possibility of healing attachment wounds independently. However, the interpersonal nature of attachment trauma often requires the safety and guidance of a therapeutic relationship to fully resolve.

Understanding your options helps you make the best choice for your healing journey:

- Self-help advantages: Accessible, affordable, allows you to work at your own pace, and provides valuable psychoeducation about attachment patterns and healing strategies
- Professional guidance benefits: Offers a corrective relational experience, provides skilled navigation through trauma responses, and creates accountability for sustained change
- Hybrid approach: Combining professional therapy with carefully chosen self-help resources maximizes both support and personal empowerment in the healing process

Nathan spent three years consuming every attachment book and podcast he could find, becoming an expert on anxious attachment theory. He could explain his patterns perfectly but still found himself spiraling into panic when his girlfriend didn't respond to texts immediately.

"I had all the knowledge but none of the embodied change," he realized.

When he finally started working with a therapist specializing in attachment, the combination of his self-education and professional guidance accelerated his progress dramatically. The therapeutic relationship itself became a laboratory for practicing secure attachment, something no book could provide.

Olivia took a different approach. Living in a rural area with limited access to specialized therapists, she created her own support system using online resources, support groups, and regular check-ins with a trusted friend who was also working on attachment healing. She supplemented this with monthly video sessions with an attachment-focused therapist.

"I had to get creative, but I found ways to get both the knowledge and the relational healing I needed," she shared.

The most important factor isn't whether you choose self-help or professional support.

It's ensuring you have some form of safe relationship to practice new attachment behaviors. Whether that's with a therapist, support group, trusted friend, or partner willing to grow alongside you, healing happens in relationship.

The 90-day program outlined in Chapter 9 can be implemented with any level of support you choose. The key is being honest about what you need to feel safe enough to change old patterns and brave enough to try new ones.

BECOMING YOUR OWN PERFECT PARENT

Reparenting involves consciously providing yourself with the emotional attunement, consistency, and unconditional love that may have been missing in childhood. This approach recognizes that healing attachment wounds requires not just understanding what went wrong, but actively experiencing what secure attachment feels like.

Three key approaches to reparenting include:

- Internal reparenting: Developing a loving, consistent internal voice that provides comfort and guidance during triggered states, replacing harsh self-criticism with compassionate support
- External reparenting experiences: Seeking out relationships and experiences that provide the safety, attunement, and consistency needed to build secure attachment templates
- Somatic reparenting: Using body-based practices to provide

your nervous system with the co-regulation and safety that supports secure attachment development

Melissa discovered reparenting when she noticed how harshly she spoke to herself during relationship conflicts. She began practicing what she called "loving parent voice"—speaking to herself the way she wished her mother had during childhood distress. When her partner seemed withdrawn, instead of her usual internal criticism ("You're being too needy again, no wonder he's pulling away"), she would offer herself compassion: "It makes sense that you're scared right now. Let's breathe together and figure out what you actually need."

This shift from self-attack to self-support gradually reduced her desperate, clingy behaviors as she learned to provide herself with the emotional security she had always sought from others.

Ryan took a different approach, focusing on external reparenting experiences. He joined a men's support group where members practiced offering each other the encouragement and validation they had missed in childhood. He also developed a relationship with a mentor who modeled secure attachment behaviors.

"Having someone consistently show up for me without judgment taught my nervous system what reliability actually felt like," he shared.

The beauty of reparenting lies in its accessibility.

You don't need to wait for the perfect therapist or partner to begin this work. Every moment offers an opportunity to treat yourself with the kindness and consistency that builds internal security.

As you experiment with different healing approaches, reparenting becomes the foundation that supports all other growth. When you can provide yourself with emotional safety, you're no longer desperately seeking it from others through clingy, anxious behaviors.

Instead, you can approach relationships from a place of wholeness rather than neediness.

9
THE PRACTICE COURTROOM - 90 DAYS OF REWIRING YOUR LOVE LIFE

DAY 89 BREAKTHROUGH IN THE MIRROR

Think of these 90 days as your practice courtroom where you're both the attorney and the judge, building your case for lasting love through evidence-based change rather than hope alone. This isn't about perfection; it's about progression through structured practice that rewires your attachment patterns at the neurological level.

Week 1-30: Foundation Building - Self-awareness vs. self-obsession

The first 30 days focus on developing healthy self-awareness without falling into the trap of narcissistic self-obsession that actually increases anxiety. True self-awareness creates emotional peace by helping you understand your patterns without judgment, while self-obsession keeps you trapped in the exhausting cycle of overthinking every interaction.

- Mindful observation without analysis paralysis: Notice your thoughts and feelings without immediately trying to fix or understand them completely
- Pattern recognition over pattern judgment: Identify your attachment triggers and responses as data points rather than character flaws
- Present-moment anchoring techniques: Develop skills to ground yourself when anxiety spirals begin, preventing the overthinking that destroys emotional peace

Beatrice started her 90-day journey convinced that constant self-analysis was the path to growth. She journaled obsessively about every interaction with her partner, dissecting conversations for hidden meanings. By day 20, she realized this "self-awareness" was actually self-torture.

Her breakthrough came when she shifted from asking "What does this mean about me?" to simply observing "I'm feeling anxious right now, and that's okay."

This subtle change transformed her relationship with her own emotions and stopped the cycle of exhausting overthinking that had plagued her for years.

Building on the experiments from Chapter 8, this phase introduces structured daily practices. Your morning routine becomes a laboratory for testing secure attachment behaviors before facing real-world relationship challenges. Instead of diving into deep emotional work immediately, you're creating a foundation of emotional stability through consistent, small actions.

The neuroscience research from Chapter 2 shows us that repetition creates neural pathways. These first 30 days aren't about dramatic revelations but about laying groundwork for sustainable change. You're training your brain to default to secure responses rather than anxious reactions through deliberate daily practice that builds emotional resilience over time.

BREAKING PATTERNS THROUGH ACTION OVER ANALYSIS

The middle phase emphasizes taking action to interrupt old patterns rather than just understanding them intellectually. While insights are valuable, behavioral change is what transforms you from clingy and desperate to confidently secure in relationships. This is where you begin practicing new responses in real-time.

Building on the experiments from Chapter 8, you're now moving beyond laboratory conditions into actual relationship challenges. The neuroscience research from Chapter 2 shows us that behavioral repetition creates lasting neural changes, but only when we actively choose different responses during moments of activation.

- The pause-and-pivot technique: Create space between trigger and response to choose security-based actions over anxiety-driven reactions
- Opposite action exercises: Deliberately practice behaviors that contradict your anxious impulses, building new neural pathways
- Confidence-building through evidence collection: Document moments when you successfully chose secure responses, creating a foundation of proof for your growing emotional strength

Ian had always been the type to send multiple texts when his partner didn't respond quickly. During week 45 of his practice, he felt the familiar urge to send a third follow-up message. Instead of acting on impulse, he used the pause-and-pivot technique: he acknowledged the anxiety, reminded himself that secure people trust their partners, and chose to go for a walk instead.

When his girlfriend called him that evening—she'd been in back-to-back meetings—he felt a surge of pride in his new response pattern.

This wasn't just insight; it was behavioral proof that he could act from confidence rather than desperation.

The digital desperation patterns we explored in Chapter 3 require this kind of active interruption. Your brain has been trained to seek immediate reassurance through texts, calls, and constant communication. Breaking these patterns means tolerating the discomfort of not knowing while choosing trust over control.

Remember the fear factory from Chapter 4 that manufactures abandonment scenarios from normal relationship moments? This phase teaches you to recognize when your mind starts producing these stories and choose different actions despite the emotional noise. You're not trying to stop the thoughts; you're learning to act independently of them.

This behavioral approach sets the foundation for Chapter 10, where you'll design sustainable relationship patterns based on security rather than anxiety. Each successful pivot creates evidence that secure attachment is possible for you.

FROM PRACTICE ARENA TO REAL BATTLEGROUND

The final phase moves beyond controlled exercises to testing your new patterns in increasingly challenging real-world situations. This is where you build genuine intimacy without fear of abandonment or losing yourself, because you've developed the skills to maintain your center regardless of external circumstances.

Drawing from the experimental foundation established in Chapter 8, you're now ready to face the intimacy challenges we explored in

Chapter 5 with new tools and confidence. The people-pleasing patterns from Chapter 6 will be tested as you learn to maintain authenticity while deepening connection.

- Graduated exposure to relationship challenges: Progressively handle more complex situations using your new secure responses
- Intimacy without losing identity: Practice deepening connection while maintaining your individual boundaries and sense of self
- Conflict as connection opportunity: Transform disagreements from threats to intimacy into chances to demonstrate your secure attachment skills

Sophia faced her biggest test during week 78 when her partner needed space to deal with a family crisis. The old version of herself would have panicked, assuming this meant rejection. Instead, she drew on 11 weeks of practice to offer genuine support while maintaining her own emotional stability.

She continued her own activities, sent one caring message per day without expecting immediate responses, and trusted that their connection could withstand this temporary distance.

When her partner returned emotionally available a week later, expressing gratitude for her support, she realized she had successfully built genuine intimacy without losing herself in the process.

This phase requires everything you've learned about partner selection from Chapter 7. You're no longer attracted to partners who trigger your anxious patterns because you've rewired your attachment system to recognize genuine compatibility over familiar chaos. The archaeological work from Chapter 1 has shown you how past wounds shaped your relationship patterns, but now you're creating new patterns based on security rather than survival.

The neuroscience courtroom from Chapter 2 demonstrates that your brain has literally changed through consistent practice. The fear factory from Chapter 4 may still occasionally produce abandonment scenarios, but you now have evidence-based responses that prevent these thoughts from controlling your behavior.

As you prepare for Chapter 10's relationship constitution, you're moving from practicing security to embodying it. These final weeks create the foundation for sustainable intimacy patterns that will serve you for years to come.

CLOCKWORK MIND MEETS WILD HEART

The most effective approach combines structured daily practices with the flexibility to respond intuitively to each day's unique challenges. Structure provides the foundation for change, while intuitive flexibility ensures you're developing authentic responses rather than rigid scripts.

- Non-negotiable daily anchors: Establish 2-3 consistent practices (like morning mindfulness or evening reflection) that reinforce secure attachment regardless of daily chaos
- Adaptive practice selection: Choose additional exercises based on current challenges, whether that's boundary work, communication skills, or anxiety management
- Integration checkpoints: Regular assessment of which practices are creating lasting change versus which might need adjustment or replacement

The key insight here is that structure serves intuition, not the other way around. Your daily anchors create the emotional stability that allows you to respond authentically rather than reactively to relationship challenges.

Recap of Key Points

The 90-day practice courtroom provides a structured yet flexible framework for transforming your love life through evidence-based change. The first 30 days build self-awareness without self-obsession, stopping the exhausting cycle of overthinking through mindful observation and present-moment anchoring. Days 31-60 focus on behavioral pattern interruption, transforming you from clingy and desperate to confidently secure through deliberate practice of new responses. The final 30 days integrate these skills in real-world testing, enabling you to build genuine intimacy without fear of abandonment or losing yourself. Throughout all phases, combining structured daily practices with intuitive flexibility ensures authentic rather than scripted growth.

Action Steps

- Choose your 90-day start date and commit to the full journey, understanding that transformation requires consistent practice over time
- Identify your top three attachment triggers and design specific practice responses for each one
- Establish 2-3 non-negotiable daily practices that you can maintain regardless of external circumstances
- Create a simple tracking system to document your progress and celebrate small wins along the way
- Find one person who can provide accountability and support throughout your 90-day commitment

While the 90-day practice courtroom provides the framework for transformation, the real test comes in designing sustainable patterns that will serve you long beyond these initial three months. In the next chapter, we'll create your personal relationship constitution—a blueprint for secure love that integrates everything you've learned into a lasting framework for intimacy without anxiety.

10

THE FUTURE RELATIONSHIP CONSTITUTION - DESIGNING YOUR SECURE TOMORROW

REDESIGNING LOVE FROM SCRATCH

The journey from anxious attachment to secure connection isn't just about healing old wounds; it's about consciously creating new patterns. Like architects designing a building meant to withstand earthquakes, securely attached couples don't leave their relationship's foundation to chance. They create what we might call a "relationship constitution"—a living document of agreements, practices, and principles that guide their partnership toward lasting security and intimacy.

The New Relationship Rules: Conscious Agreements vs. Organic Evolution

Most relationships operate on unspoken assumptions and inherited patterns from past experiences or family dynamics. Secure relationships, however, thrive on conscious agreements—explicit understandings about how partners want to show up for each other and navigate their shared life.

- Explicit Boundary Setting: Rather than expecting partners to read minds or guess preferences, secure couples articulate their needs, limits, and non-negotiables clearly. This includes everything from communication styles to physical affection preferences to financial decisions.
- Regular Relationship Check-ins: Scheduled conversations (weekly, monthly, or quarterly) where partners assess how their agreements are working, what needs adjustment, and what new challenges require attention. These aren't crisis meetings but preventive maintenance for the relationship.
- Values Alignment Documentation: Writing down shared values and individual values, then creating agreements about how to honor both. This prevents the common anxious pattern of losing oneself in the relationship while also avoiding the avoidant tendency to maintain rigid independence.

Austin and his partner discovered this approach after a near-breakup caused by completely different assumptions about social media boundaries. He assumed privacy meant not posting couple photos, while his partner interpreted this as shame about the relationship. Their "social media agreement" became their first conscious contract, specifying how they wanted to represent their relationship online.

This single conversation prevented months of overthinking and misinterpretation.

The success of this one agreement led them to create conscious agreements about everything from household responsibilities to career support, transforming their dynamic from reactive to proactive. Instead of waiting for problems to emerge organically, they began designing solutions before conflicts arose. This approach eliminated the guesswork that previously triggered Austin's anxious spirals and created the predictable security both partners needed to thrive.

SCRIPTS OR SPARKS IN CONVERSATION

While spontaneous communication has its place, secure relationships benefit from having structured approaches to important conversations. These protocols ensure both partners feel heard and prevent discussions from escalating into destructive patterns that trigger anxious attachment responses.

Remember the neuroscience we explored in Chapter 2—when your amygdala hijacks rational thinking, having predetermined structures becomes your lifeline back to secure communication.

Communication Protocols That Work

- The 24-Hour Rule: For significant concerns or conflicts, partners agree to take at least 24 hours to process before having the conversation. This prevents reactive communication and allows for thoughtful responses rather than defensive reactions that fuel the fear factory we discussed in Chapter 4.
- Speaker-Listener Format: During important discussions, one person speaks while the other listens without interrupting, then reflects back what they heard before responding. This simple structure eliminates the exhausting cycle of talking past each other that often triggers abandonment fears.
- Emotion Before Content: Partners share their emotional state before diving into the topic at hand. Starting with "I'm feeling anxious about this conversation" or "I'm excited to share this with you" sets the tone and helps the listener respond appropriately.

These aren't rigid scripts that kill spontaneity—they're safety nets that allow deeper intimacy to flourish.

From Text Message Tribunal to Clear Communication

Chloe used to spend hours analyzing every text message from her partner, wondering if his brief responses meant he was pulling away. Their communication protocol now includes a simple check-in system where each person can request clarity about tone or intention without judgment. When his texts seem short, instead of spiraling into overthinking, she simply asks, "Are you feeling rushed, or is everything okay?"

This direct approach eliminated ninety percent of her relationship anxiety.

The transformation happened gradually during her ninety-day rewiring process from Chapter 9. She discovered that her partner actually appreciated these check-ins because they prevented misunderstandings that had previously led to unnecessary conflicts. What started as her anxious need for reassurance evolved into a mutual communication tool that strengthened their connection.

This protocol helped her build the confidence to address concerns immediately rather than letting them fester into the catastrophic scenarios her anxious mind typically created.

BUILDING BRIDGES BEFORE THEY BURN

Secure relationships don't avoid conflict—they have systems for navigating disagreements that strengthen rather than damage the connection. These couples invest equally in preventing unnecessary conflicts and repairing effectively when conflicts do arise.

This approach directly counters the fear factory mentality we explored in Chapter 4, where every disagreement feels like a relationship-ending catastrophe.

Conflict Navigation Systems

- The Conflict Pause Protocol: When emotions escalate beyond productive levels, either partner can call for a pause without it being seen as avoidance or abandonment. They agree on a specific timeframe to reconvene (usually thirty minutes to twenty-four hours) and both commit to self-soothing during the break.
- Repair Rituals: Specific actions or phrases that help restore connection after disagreements. These might include physical gestures, verbal affirmations, or shared activities that remind both partners of their underlying bond and commitment to the relationship.
- The 80/20 Rule: Understanding that in most conflicts, both partners contribute something to the dynamic. Even if one person is eighty percent responsible, the other partner examines their twenty percent contribution without defensiveness, focusing on their part rather than keeping score.

These systems transform conflict from a threat into an opportunity for deeper understanding.

From Fear to Connection Through Repair

Marcus and his partner developed what they call their "reset ritual" after discovering that their post-conflict repair attempts often felt awkward and forced. Now, after any significant disagreement, they take turns sharing one thing they appreciated about how the other person handled the conflict and one thing they want to do differently next time.

This ritual helps them build genuine intimacy without the fear of abandonment that used to follow every argument.

The transformation took months of practice from his ninety-day rewiring process in Chapter 9. Initially, Marcus would spiral after conflicts, convinced that every disagreement meant his partner was planning to leave. The reset ritual gave him concrete evidence that conflicts could actually bring them closer together rather than drive them apart.

Instead of walking on eggshells after disagreements, they now feel closer and more secure in their ability to weather future storms together. What once triggered his abandonment fears now strengthens their bond and builds confidence in their relationship's resilience.

FINDING YOUR SWEET SPOT BETWEEN INDEPENDENCE AND TOGETHERNESS

The secure relationship constitution explicitly addresses the balance between individual identity and couple identity. Rather than swinging between enmeshment and disconnection, partners create agreements that honor both their need for togetherness and their need for separateness.

This directly counters the people-pleasing patterns we examined in Chapter 6, where losing yourself becomes the price of keeping someone else.

Interdependence Agreements

- Individual Growth Budgets: Time, energy, and financial resources allocated to each partner's personal development, hobbies, friendships, and individual goals. This prevents the resentment that builds when one or both partners sacrifice their identity for the relationship.
- Couple Rituals and Traditions: Regularly scheduled activities that belong uniquely to the partnership—weekly

date nights, annual trips, daily check-ins, or seasonal traditions that strengthen the couple's bond and shared identity.

- Friend and Family Integration Agreements: Clear understandings about how much time to spend with extended social networks, how to handle conflicting loyalties, and how to present a united front while maintaining individual relationships.

These agreements eliminate the guesswork that typically triggers anxious spirals about whether you're being too needy or too distant.

From Clingy to Confidently Interdependent

Isabella realized she had been trying to transform from clingy and desperate to confidently secure by swinging too far toward independence. Her new relationship constitution includes what she calls "interdependence agreements"—specific ways she and her partner support each other's individual goals while building their shared life.

For example, they each get two evenings per week for individual pursuits, but they also commit to one weekly activity that's just for them as a couple.

This structure gives her the security of knowing their connection is prioritized while also ensuring she maintains her individual identity and interests. The framework eliminated her constant worry about whether she was asking for too much attention or not giving enough space.

During her ninety-day rewiring process from Chapter 9, Isabella discovered that having explicit agreements about togetherness and separateness actually increased her confidence in both areas. She could pursue her painting hobby without guilt because it was part of their agreed-upon individual growth budget. She could also request couple time without feeling needy because their weekly date was a mutual commitment, not her desperate attempt to manufacture connection.

CONCLUSION

You picked up this book because you were tired. Tired of the exhausting cycle of overthinking every interaction, analyzing every text message, and losing sleep over what someone might be thinking or feeling. You were ready to stop the emotional rollercoaster that left you feeling clingy and desperate, always on edge about whether you were too much or not enough.

The vision we've explored together throughout these pages is both simple and profound: you can transform from anxious attachment patterns to secure, confident relating. This isn't about becoming a different person—it's about becoming the most authentic, grounded version of yourself. It's about finally experiencing the emotional peace you've been seeking and building genuine intimacy without the constant fear of abandonment or losing yourself in the process.

This transformation happens through three essential phases. First, understanding your past—not to blame or remain stuck, but to recognize how your early experiences shaped your nervous system and relationship patterns. Second, rewiring your present through consistent, intentional practices that literally change your brain's default responses. And third, consciously creating your relationship future by making daily choices that align with security rather than anxiety.

The journey from anxious to secure attachment is ultimately about reclaiming your power.

Throughout our ten chapters together, you've discovered that your anxious attachment stems from early adaptive strategies. Your nervous system learned to be hypervigilant and seek constant reassurance because, at some point in your development, this was the best strategy available for getting your needs met. These patterns made sense in their original context, even if they're causing problems now.

You've learned that your brain can be rewired through consistent practice. Neuroplasticity means your brain remains changeable throughout your lifetime. The neural pathways that fire together wire together, so by repeatedly choosing secure responses over anxious ones, you literally reshape your brain's default patterns.

Perhaps most importantly, you've discovered that your attachment style is changeable, not fixed. One of the most liberating realizations is that attachment styles are not permanent personality traits carved in stone. They are learned patterns of relating that can be unlearned and replaced with healthier ones. Your past does not determine your future—your daily choices do.

You've also learned to distinguish between anxiety and intuition. Anxious attachment can make you believe that your worried thoughts and catastrophic predictions are actually intuitive insights. True intuition doesn't create panic; it provides clarity. When you're spinning in anxious thoughts, you're not accessing wisdom—you're accessing old wounds.

Most crucially, you now understand that you deserve love without having to earn it. Perhaps the most profound shift in moving from anxious to secure attachment is recognizing that love is not something you earn through perfect behavior, constant giving, or making yourself indispensable. You are inherently worthy of love simply by existing.

Your journey toward secure attachment doesn't end with closing this book—it begins there. Here's your roadmap for the next 90 days:

- Begin your 90-day journey today: Commit to 90 days of intentional practice and choose three specific techniques from this book to practice daily
- Find a practice partner or therapist: Healing happens in relationship, so identify someone who can support your growth journey
- Track your progress daily: Keep a simple log of your emotional state, triggers, responses, and lessons learned
- Celebrate small wins: Acknowledge every step forward, no matter how minor it might seem

As we reach the end of our journey together, I want you to know something important: your anxious attachment developed to protect you. The hypervigilance, the people-pleasing, the constant worry about relationships—these were your nervous system's best attempts to keep you safe and connected when you were most vulnerable.

That anxious part of you deserves gratitude, not criticism.

But now you're strong enough to choose something different. You have the awareness, tools, and support to transform from clingy and desperate to confidently secure in relationships. The exhausting cycle of overthinking every interaction can finally come to an end, replaced by the emotional peace you've been seeking.

The love you've always wanted is waiting on the other side of your willingness to heal. It's not the dramatic, anxiety-provoking intensity that you might have mistaken for passion in the past. It's something far more valuable: a love that feels like coming home to yourself.

The transformation begins now, with your very next choice.

Choose security. Choose peace. Choose yourself.

www.ingramcontent.com/pod-product-compliance
Lightning Source LLC
LaVergne TN
LVHW101616210926
848480LV00009B/703

* 9 7 9 8 2 3 2 8 3 1 5 4 7 *